News from This Lonesome City

poems by

Jessica Gregg

Finishing Line Press
Georgetown, Kentucky

News from This Lonesome City

*For Baltimore, and
the two children
I raised here*

Copyright © 2019 by Jessica Gregg
ISBN 978-1-63534-976-4 First Edition
All rights reserved under International and Pan-American Copyright Conventions. No part of this book may be reproduced in any manner whatsoever without written permission from the publisher, except in the case of brief quotations embodied in critical articles and reviews.

ACKNOWLEDGMENTS

In 2009, I joined the staff of Sisters Academy of Baltimore, a middle school for girls from southwest Baltimore, and served for five years as the school's graduate support director. Although the position itself was a departure from my path as a journalist and writer, it was easily the best job I ever had as it taught me so much about work, life, and finding one's purpose. Many of the observations I make about Baltimore in these poems come directly from that time. I was privileged to be a part of that community and am indebted to Sister Virginia Brune, Sister Delia Dowling, and Sister Debbie Liesen for mentoring me, and to the teachers, parents, and students who likewise taught me so much.

These poems began as work in a prose poetry class through Johns Hopkins University's Odyssey program. Thank you to our instructor, Shane Moritz, and my fellow writers, Jennifer Dowdell, Dan Dudrow, Rachel Glick, and Kimberly Leith, who continued to support me after that class ended through a monthly poetry group that was always both insightful and inspirational. You made me a better writer.

Thank you to Erica Dawson for her guidance and inspiration. Finally, a big shout out to David Stuck who took the cover photo and is one of the many colleagues of mine who makes it a joy to come to work every day.

Publisher: Leah Maines
Editor: Christen Kincaid
Cover Art: David Stuck
Author Photo: David Stuck
Cover Design: Elizabeth Maines McCleavy

Printed in the USA on acid-free paper.
Order online: www.finishinglinepress.com
also available on amazon.com

Author inquiries and mail orders:
Finishing Line Press
P. O. Box 1626
Georgetown, Kentucky 40324
U. S. A.

Table of Contents

Headlines

Dispatch 1
Last Gasps of White Men 2
Last Thoughts 5
Missing 6
Black Backpack 8
How to Talk to the Loved Ones 9
News from This Lonesome City 10

Lives

Photo of the Week 13
Phone Call 14
A feminist clarifies 15
What the Museum Placard Failed to Say
 About the Artist's Wife 16
Sandvika 17
Legend 18
Pact 19

Scores

Diamonds 23
875 North Michigan Avenue 24
To Read 25
#SpinCycle 26
The Look They Had 28
Lizards 29
To the Spies on Facebook 30
ted koppel warned us 31
This town is dead 32

Headlines

Dispatch

They sent her to cover the disappearance of
our world. In a borrowed parka and boots,
she pick axed her way

upon moon marsh ground, unsteady feet,
surefire adrenaline. Later, she thought, she
could brag about these dangers.

She packed vials for artifacts, cameras
for proof, a compass, dog whistles,
notebooks, First Aid, fertility beads.

How does one lure and then pin absence
under a glass, or trap nothing in a jar?
What is the end?

There were details for her story:
Helicopters circling, canons thumping.
Human effort charged the air.

On the ledge above the sea change surge
she peered into the crevasse, her prize
destiny slivered between the rocks.

She longed for this big bang powder keg.
Glinting bits. Tiny hits of star dust.
We are all made of star stuff.

Now we glitter.

In the dark pools of world weary tears, shed skin,
she inhaled the great breath of gone and saw
everything and nothing and herself.

Last Gasps of White Men

I

They set their GPS to ghetto-avoid, but one day a
girl in the projects made that her hot wire project.
Suddenly their BMWs brought them here.

Blinkety blink, squint eyed, blue light disbelief.
The police put those lights so close to our homes—
we don't need night lights. The moon glow

shone on their skin and they counted us all up.
Gold-hooped goodness, we flanked in rank
and stared back. National Geographic special.

Long after they had forgotten about this city,
we stitched down the streets and kept
them from rolling back into the earth.

We grew the concrete roses and lettuce leaves
Vacuumed up the moon dust, cloud tears
Counted up the houses, the children, the ghosts

We were the records, artifacts, historians,
the proof of the civilization that once was here.
They ran to the shiny, the easy. We held our

elders' hands and closed their eyelids. To pioneer is
to achieve. To patchwork is to be poor. Hundred years
ago, we were the umbrella capital of the world.

Stand close, this looks like a skeleton. But once I
open its canopy, you will see how well it keeps
the rain off that nice leather coat.

II

The woman in the store didn't like him. He knew it.
To get on her good side, he stacked the colds first,
yogurt, green pepper, guacamole. Followed by

Crackers, tea bags, the bread last. She even didn't
look at him when she gave him his change. As he left,
he saw her sugar talk the woman behind him.

High fiving about the weather, she traded out
that near-perfect melon for a better one.

This was how it started. Soon enough,
he and the others would have to move to
secondhand cities, set up their own shops,

Grow their own tomatoes, start their own stores.
They would be left behind, any time now, discarded
and forsaken, to take care of themselves.

III

In the backyard of her rowhouse between
heirlooms and black-eyeds she grew
the mold that became vaccine.

Tiny nothing becomes something becomes
Indispensable. How did we survive before?
Ambition is always the brightest star on days

into nights into days, laboratories, hospital wards
tech startups, prize money. The New Entrepreneur!
Blink-eyed, caffeine-fired. When she paused to breathe

the city's thin air, it was good. Elbow to elbow, she told
him her story over gin and showed him the medals,
trophies, statues of glory, rings of honor, certificates

papers, prizes, his fingerprints lingering,
smudging. It was too much, he said in gold-filled
gold tone. Too much for just one girl, his voice

still smiling. In her black night backyard
she noticed the burnt-out bulb of sky light
and scaled the roof to change out the stars.

Last Thoughts

Like a movie, the gangsters burst in as
her love was about to change
his face/his trade/their life.

They pray to the patron saint of petrol.
But how can a baby stand guard over a man
who bleeds pipelines, carries grenades?

And what kind of hubris does it take
to cut away the cheekbones of ancestors?
Spade to rock and red clay soil

under the nails forever, it stains flesh.
Tattoos the heart, the priest says;
Blood doesn't go back in the body.

She was considering the way
the rain falls in the desert and that
she wished to be that: Rain

Even in his sleep, his hand was on her,
gun always ready, this was what it was like to
be needed, to be more indelible than fingerprints.

Now they say Mary Magdalene was
an apostle and not a whore, but she
has always known this to be true.

Of this and other things she will never be asked
Blood spent, martyred, accessorized, dismissed.
We always ask the wrong questions to the wrong people.

Missing

Maybe they fall into manholes.

Maybe the earth swallows them
up and reconstitutes their beauty
into wild scarlet-hipped roses.

Maybe they are plucked from danger
and delivered into the milky way to
diamond dazzle us with star dust.

Maybe they disappear at midnight,
along with the dress, the shoes,
the pumpkin, and the mice.

Maybe they never existed.

Maybe the angels and the saints sweep
them away from earthen purgatories.

Maybe they are goddesses
and were never meant to stay.

Maybe they are stolen by gods
to be their very playthings.

Maybe no one ever sees them really,
so it doesn't matter anyway.

Maybe they are the wrong color.

Maybe they look wrong and walk
wrong and breathe wrong.

Maybe it's all wrong.

Maybe one day they cough so long
and so loud in class the teacher calls
the social worker who calls the city.

Maybe there are bruises. Or fleas.

Maybe we pray them away.

Maybe we are just too afraid to have them.

Maybe we don't love them enough.

Maybe we love them too much.

Maybe we don't deserve them.

Maybe we'll never know.

Black Backpack

After the crime, they lined up every boy
they could find, shoulder to shoulder, this city to
next, hands across America, and searched bags.

Fingers first into life's cargo hold,
They found missing keys, missing homework.
The missing reasons why.

Black pens. Broken pens. The red pencil
that penned them in. Go here. Go there.
Take that long road and don't stop.

He was just small when he first heard about
the Highway to Nowhere and he pictured
a ramp ending in sky, a skate jump for cars.

Oh, the ultimate adrenaline, chase scene,
crash scene, jump seat, jump out—
but it was a just cattle shoot corralling

Boys like him within city blocks
their black packs sinking them with
texbooks, gym shoes, history and truth.

How to Talk to the Loved Ones

Look at any pictures they show you. Look at them again.

Apologize for why you are here.

Don't sit too comfortably on the couch. You are not a guest.

Don't take any food, no matter how many people offer it.

Shake every hand every time it's offered.

Tell them that it's OK if they don't want to talk, but it's your hope that your story isn't all about their loved one's death. (This is a line you develop, because you have to say something. Because you don't want to be one of those reporters. Because you are better than that. Because your editor has sent you there and you have to come back with something. At this moment, you are too young and too inexperienced to know that this line is actually the truth. No matter how we die, it is never all about our deaths. But it takes a friend's cancer, 9-11, your husband's depression, and a host of other tragedies great and small before you realize this.)

Bring tissues.

Don't look away. This is your job.

News from This Lonesome City

"It was the best job ever," the Uber driver says, spinning
past the fence-post skyscrapers and crosswalks of lawyers.
"It was loud. And hot. And dirty." Oh man, could he go back?

Nothing compared to steel work. It yanked my grandfather
roots up from the tobacco farm, turned him into
a welder, galvanizing his fate into battleships.

What a time! Those gold rush, street car, metal lunch
box days of double-shift overtime, double-stuffed wallets.
Supper clubs, softball games, afternoon soaps. Steel!

"Do you know you're an old soul?" The palm reader
peers into my dry hands and sees those steel beams, long
nights, war heroes. These fingers wrap around so many lives.

Sometimes I think I was born in the wrong time. I have waited
a decade for this city to sweep away its ash, mosaic its crumbled
walls into thick-skinned fists that will hide their lines from seers.

But maybe time is only a construct. Maybe I am not here, I am really
there, cards strewn in rummy, gin in a glass, blackout curtains
drawn way down in case the U-boats see this tiny, tiny static spark.

Lives

Photo of the Week

Thankfully, someone remembered that they had given away the statues when they tore down the old church to make room for the school. The Blessed Mother. Joseph the Carpenter. Angels and archangels. A communion of saints had gone to live in corncribs and garages. Or to stand watch over farmstand zucchini. In his rattling truck, he set out to retrieve them. Thrones and Dominions, dusty and dotted with pigeon crap. It was best, he thought, to drive them through the car wash before he returned them. This was as close as he ever got to God.

Phone call

"Are you the editor," she whispers. I sit up straight, the phone pressed into my cheek. "The situation has changed," she says. Then: "I can give the money back." Remorse spills out, a tipped over purse dropping tubes of lipsticks. A spare key. "What I wrote is no longer true." Quarters. Chewed bits of gum. A Kleenex. Mass card. Condoms. Words can topple out, but they can't be stuffed back in. A transaction happened. Nouns and verbs were bought and sold. But she wants to give back the money. "What I wrote had an impact I didn't expect." Oh, were that true for all of us, that the act of putting pen to paper and thought and feeling between capital letter and punctuation would transform us all! The purse is spilled in front of me, yet I ignore its contents. I am an editor-philosopher with the long view. Just for argument's sake, what are these words she wants to buy back? "Why I am sleeping with a white man," she whispers. Now what topples before me are history and race and gender and politics. And suddenly I understand how philosophy is all fine and good. So is the notebook I carry in the day to day so no words are ever lost. I hold it tight in hand, but still never zipper my purse. I am reckless like this.

A feminist clarifies

I wrote that I had not the skill to stir his soup
—and a revolt ensued.

What I meant to say was that he bargains
with musk earth for three carrots, two
potatoes, a fringe of spinach. Sweet talks
basil, sits with onions as tears are shed.
Pick-pockets the pea pods of cannellinis to cast out
their coins. Cracks BB's of pepper in his hands
oyster shell
        scatter shell
                gunshot
Dice and cut, diamond cut
spool thread, noodle crank, fusilli fresh

Soup's on, the supper man serves.

Spoon-fed, full-belly, full-love, full-up
I am shoeless, but not oppressed.

What the Museum Placard Failed to Say About the Artist's Wife

That over her bitter morning coffee she let her mind wander to the periwinkle and cerise dreams of hope.

That as a child she saw the world so much bigger than the lines in which it was drawn.

That she was the one who blunted the tangerine body of the fish and cooked it over the smoky beach pit before splaying it on the plate that the artist would paint.

That she pulled the lobster from the sea.

That she saw the way the world melted in our imperfect gaze, the way our own flaws shone from our eyes. In truth, the aubergine peaks and sanguine sun were truly untouchable.

That his paintings were her agency, her mark in the world, signed as though their blood was truly the same. That he wore her like a bone gray pearl, delighted when men turned at her cackle of laughter.

That she was not the muse.

That love is smaller than anything else, and that genius, well, genius is a pencil line on the edge of the page.

Sandvika

In bright light December, we tinsel bravery and dare nature,
candlelight our windowpanes and glow.
But the artist came in February when the only colors
of winter were wait and white, edgeless landscapes
with no corners to grab, nor color to footprint on canvas.
We wait at the train station, the whole town hoping to be
the one to carry his satchel that will unfurl water lilies
through our emptiness. Floral borealis. Cold burns the eyes.
Freezes our breath to beard. Shovels glint. Everything echoes.
A thicket of fur. My thick fingers can't curl around a brush.
My eyes see ice, not blue-rippled dreams of mercy.
But feet, my feet set steady guide, and he follows my trail.
I lead, he follows. On this lone day, I sketch and he colors
my town. My beautiful heart dances in the snowy light.
I will record this for my children's children. He is a master.

Legend

Large deeds speak of large love.
He harnessed the house to a team
of horses to drag across the ice.
Here is my heart.

Of course, it would have been
easier to raise their own beams.
But why must we be ordinary?
What is left of us in the end

But the stories that are told?
Words linger longer than walls
and foundation. Even now,
I can hear the crack of ice

Feel his sinking love in my own chest.
Submerged, hope floats.
Not a feather, but whispers
we repeat to each other.

Pact

They found the baby in the parking lot, wrapped in a bed quilt. Button of warm in a bundle too big. Pretty baby. The cops came to ask them what they knew.

Don't drink the water around here, the girls had told her on her first day. Laughing. She didn't understand their warning.

It rained a lot that spring, corn grew like crazy. The kitchen had no windows, but they could still smell the storms.

They washed dishes, poured coffee, played cards on break. One by one, their bellies swelled. Blossom-perfect fecundity.

Truth told, she wasn't like them. Nothing rolled easy with her, but maybe, it didn't matter if you stood close enough to danger.

What she wanted was to always put away the dishes together, like they were in their own kitchen. Like they were sisters. Like she wasn't so afraid.

A pinwheel spins in the garden. Eight triangles make one quilt block, alternating colors, light and dark, light and dark. It's one of the oldest patterns.

Scores

Diamonds

He made the drive in for the baseball game
and brought her ex-boyfriend,
the woman whose husband had groped her,
and the man she had cut off last week in Remington.

They hunkered in the bleachers, a team of
aggrieved and agitated, regulation chip on their
shoulders. They nicked a scorecard, bought
hot dogs from the boosters, and yelled at the umpire.

Chanting and calling out, they threw French fries at her,
blaming her every time the wind took the ball. Then they led the
crowd in a wave of fury, sparking the old wooden seats with a
rage that nettled her in its undercurrent.

She dropped down, deep down into the secret river silt of
Blackburne fame, destined to be thrown glory in the
Big League, or perhaps turned edge by edge from the
heat and friction into pure black carbonado.

875 North Michigan Avenue

Morning news item: The owners of Chicago's former John Hancock Building are now accepting bids for the rights to name this iconic skyscraper.

The Building Formerly Known as Hancock
Hancock Heresy
Hancock Hereafter
Herbie Hancock
Hands Cocked to the Sky, Beseeching
Hands Cocked to the Sky, Celebrating
Cockamamie
Chicago's Finest
The Former Insurance Tower
A Big Pen for Your Signature
Ball Point Tower
Finger Tower
Finger to the Sky
Big, Pointy Building
Tally, McTall Tower
Celestial Popsicle
Ambition in 100 Floors
Rocket to Venus
Tower of Ambition
Tower of Hope
Tall Tower Two
Greatest Generation Tower
Space Age Tower
1976 Tower
When We Believed Building
A Building Beyond Our Dreams
When We Aim for Immortality
Immortality Artifact
Our Fingerprint in a Finger Point
The Here We Were Skyscraper
This Was Our Building

To Read

7 Easy-To-Make Meals
10 Must-Read Titles
14 Exercises to Try Now
23 Ways to Relax
25 Mantras to Counter Your Hateful Coworkers
31 Breathing Techniques
37 Ways Your Slow Cooker Can Clean Your House
41 Strategies to Simplify Your Life
56 Sex Moves to Try Now
61 Things You Can Think, But Shouldn't Say
64 House Hacks
72 Ways to Exercise in the Elevator Parking Garage
78 Organizational Tips
82 Films to Watch
87 Things We Forget About Our Friends
95 Songs for Your Summer Playlist
105 Health Tests to Know About
109 Times You Will Question Yourself This Week
117 Ways to Stop Time and Pin It, Like a Dead Butterfly, Into a Scrapbook
123 Strategies to Prove You Existed
117 New Beauty Products to Try Today
132 Reminders That You Are But a Small Speck in This Vast, Bone-Breaking Universe
147 Ways to Breathe

#SpinCycle

@justanotherhero where's the
hurricane party? or is everybody out
buying toilet paper???

sad state of affairs when the most
interesting thing to watch is the weather
#thiscountryisboring

meteorologists have it made
#moneyfornothing
#iwantthatjob

home alone and no one is making
a movie about it. #5thingsaboutme
i am watching the weather

deadiest hurricane ever Galveston 1900
#mediasaveslives they keep saying
storm surge is most dangerous #deadisdead

seagulls over parking lot mean snow
except if you live in Kansas
#weirdsuperstitions

what would happen if this storm turned right
now and came right toward us?
#ruready?

remember when they said the stock exchange
was flooded? #hurricanesandy
#thenewsismadeup

there was more than one shooter
in dallas #thenewsismadeup
they killed his mistress too

#5thingsaboutme still watching the weather
hurricane katrina was the costliest
#bandsofrainisnotametalgroup

so many people donated food that it had
to be thrown out #crazywaste they hate
the poor but send them soda #iwantabiggulp

shirts off their back #doublestandard
mental picture: astronauts shaking their head
at us now #werscrewed #godspeedjohnglenn

i'm just a kid on twitter don't ask me how these
things happen warm air rises quickly into cold air
a spiral is created #ipassedscience

there is a storm there is an eye there is wind
to push it along then there is all of us watching
power off #hurricane

The Look They Had

for Isaac Asimov, for writing "The Fun They Had"

She was in the subway when she first saw the face.
Spectacular for its irregularity! Wide forehead,
long nose with a pointy peak of cartilage.

She had seen photos of relatives before feature selection.
Oh, there were all sorts of riotous, rough-edged anatomy!
Narrow-hole eyes. Lopsided smiles. Ears that hung down

like wet shirts on a laundry line. Stiff-plank teeth.
Copper-coil hair. Wire-brush hair. Silt-fine hair.
Hair on lips on chins in noses in ears.

It was so easy to tell them apart. There's a chinless uncle,
a cousin with dimples. So easy!
Thank, god, right? They didn't have chips.

No, they had destiny cheeks, celestial hips,
chance-made knees, arms, arches. Bulbous beautiful bodies.
Freckled fantasia. Pock-marked perfection.

Simpler lives.

Lizards

The lizards appeared in January, when black branches wired the city beneath a gray lidded sky. Bleak, but not cold. Imposter winter. Then, these creatures.

They crawled from a crack between rowhouses, green palm fronds hurtling themselves on the living room floor until it became a moss carpet. A pulsing rug of reptiles. An impossible story.

Theories weed spread down alleys and through back doors.
It was a hoax. They were all toys. It was a joke. A pet store prank.

How could such delicate life, such cold-blooded, rubber-skinned creatures, find refuge in this concrete-edged town? Reporters, scientists, bookies, bloggers. T-shirt makers and witnesses all showed up.

This is proof we have grown too much and we live where we shouldn't. We have taken over the lizard habitat!

This is proof the planet is changing and confused lizards see this urban desert as home!

This is proof in God, magnanimous and whimsical, who rains life on our colorless world. When we thought we couldn't go on, they came!

This is proof there are lizards. Cracks in concrete. Things hidden. Endings we don't know. I want to run my fingers over the scar that birthed them. Mostly, I want to stretch on this floor and see what they see. Their tread is a whisper as they settle into this new home.

To the Spies on Facebook

I don't pray. I have insomnia, toenail fungus (on one lone nail), uneven eyebrows. Today, I Googled hurricane season, African penguins, Chadwick Boseman, and the artist pants from American Eagle.

I should have had more children.

And I am old enough to remember Sting's Soviet song.

My people are nostalgic for whirring factories, smokestacks, steel stacks, long haul trains, myths we stitched and stamped. But it's no secret-group secret there's no loving cup champagne, love-your-neighbor, love our future, shiny scrapers here. No Golden Miles, Fords in the driveway, super in our power, I fear. But you don't get a medal for figuring this out.

We are a fading Colosseum and I have the food ready for the stray cats. Run along.

ted koppel warned us

the attack will be soundless
our gasps the only commotion
what we think is the draining of our souls
is the last bars of our cell phones

how many batteries do we need?
how many protein bars?

they say 9 months   the gestation of a child
no lights   no tv   no alexa   no atm

will we cannibal our suburbs to heat our homes
with ikea shelves? guard our particle board and
generators with bared teeth and guns?

when my girl was a baby i had to hold
her upright in the night so she wouldn't choke
tiny body   one mother   night's deep pocket

i thought of my grandmother then, cycles of life
she still hid money in the ceiling joints even
after the great depression ended

she would tell us now to trust ted

i want to believe her i want to believe we will
play cards by candlelight and turn our sod lawns
into thickets of sweet pea while we wait for the army

This town is dead

This town is dead.

The clubs are closed, but see this scrap of red carpet?
Let me roll it under your feet.

My playlist is full and these rowhouse walls are thick.

People were born here and people died here. Their blood
thumps base. That drum is my heart. I am more steady
than I look. Toe tap. Thwap. Rap. My feet don't know quiet.

Funny, because I kept my mouth on silent for years. Lock and zipper.
When the planes flew over, I never called 911. If you don't say
it out loud, no one can take it from you.

You hear that song? Turn it up louder. Take off your shoes. We dance
up. Cut up. Stay up. Sway through.

We were left for dead. But we fooled them.

Jessica Gregg is editor of *Baltimore's Child, Washington Family* and *Baltimore Style* magazines. She is a former educator who lives in a rowhouse on the edge of Baltimore. Her children are the fifth generation of her family to live in that house.

www.ingramcontent.com/pod-product-compliance
Lightning Source LLC
LaVergne TN
LVHW041602070426
835507LV00011B/1265